Delaisa

Delaisa

CALANI CADENCE AMORY

Calani Cadence Amory
Delaisa

Published by Spines
ISBN 979-8-89691-049-7

Contents

Prologue

THE TIME - PRESENT DAY

THE PLACE – DELAISA.

Delaisa was a most picturesque town by the sea. There were several boats and yachts that bobbed up and down on the water. One of the yachts belonged to Dante Cecchi. The people of Delaisa were quite friendly. They all looked out for each other. Delaisa was warm in the summer and cold in the winter. The pretty time of year was in spring. That was when the little crocuses started to peep out their little heads. Little green buds started to sprout on the trees.

Dante Cecchi sat at his desk. It was the start of what he expected would be another long day. He stood up and went over to the coffee machine. As he sipped his coffee, he looked up at the sky. It was a dark steel gray. As a financial advisor, he was used to working long hours. He took small comfort in the fact that it was Friday. He was already planning his weekend.

Back at his desk, he looked over his schedule for the day. He had meetings all day. It seemed like he spent his life in meetings. Dante had always been extremely driven. He knew what he wanted in life and went after his dreams.

Chapter Two

It was just after eight in the evening when Dante decided to call it a day. After the long hours, he was quite tired. All he wanted was to go home and relax with a nice hot meal. As soon as he stepped outside, he could feel a chill in the air. The temperature had dropped significantly since the last time he was outside. The night was turning misty, and the full moon was drifting in and out of the clouds. In the distance he heard a dog bark.

As he was driving home, he was pleased to see that traffic was light. In twenty minutes, he was home. After a nice hot meal, he went into his home office. While at his desk, he checked his emails. There was one from his father about the upcoming gala. Dante Cecchi was an all-around good guy. He enjoyed taking care of his parents and two younger sisters, Chiara and Marisa.

He walked into his living room and looked around. After being there for the past few years, he decided it was time for him to consider moving.

Chapter Three

On this Friday night, Mateo Vicente and Francisco Valencia were enjoying a friendly game of pool in Mateo's basement. As Francisco was positioning himself to take a shot, Mateo said "there is no way you can make that." Francisco glanced quickly at Mateo and said, "oh yeah? watch me." he hit the ball, and it went into the hole. He stood up and took a bow. Mateo said, "you just got lucky." Francisco said, "I'm just good." Mateo and Francisco had been friends since high school. Their fathers had worked together. Just then the lights went out for a quick minute. When they came back on, Francisco said "I do believe I should head out now." Mateo said, "I believe you're right." not long after Francisco left, the lights went out once more. Suddenly there was a loud clap of thunder.

Bright and early on Saturday morning, Natalia Rivera was bustling around her boutique, busily getting ready for the day ahead. As she expected it would be a busy day, she had scheduled extra help. Being quite ambitious, it had always been her dream to have her own boutique. While she was in college, she had studied business and fashion. After the passing of her beloved grandfather, she had inherited a generous sum of money. She had used some of that money to open her boutique. Now after six months, she was doing quite well. One of the contributing factors to her success was the location. Natalia had a great eye for fashion, and she had great business smarts. Her boutique was nestled between the beauty salon and the barber shop. The joke around town was that when one wanted to hear the latest juicy gossip, one just had to walk into the beauty salon or the barber shop.

On Sunday afternoon, Dante was enjoying a late brunch with his parents, Carlo and Evelina. It had been a while since he had spent some time with them. The sun was high and glistened on the turquoise water of the pool. Evelina said to Dante "It's so nice to have you over." Carlo, seated beside her nodded in agreement. Dante said "I know. I've been busy with work." just then his two younger sisters, Chiara and Marisa arrived. Chiara was the younger of the two and was quite feisty. She had just finished writing her first book and was looking for a publisher. She said, "yeah busy with your girlfriend." Dante looked at her and frowned and Chiara giggled. Marisa just opened her first boutique and was doing quite well. Evelina said to both girls "It's about time you two arrived." Marisa said, "I wanted to show Chiara my new boutique." Carlo smiled and said "that's fantastic. Good for you Marisa." Evelina asked

Chiara “any luck finding a publisher, Cici?” Chiara sat beside Marisa and said “no, not yet.” Dante said, “I am sure you will find one soon.” Chiara said, “I hope so.” just then there was a loud clap of thunder. All of them jumped up and went inside. An hour later, Dante, Chiara and Marisa left.

Chapter Six

Across town, Ricardo Ortiz and Julian Cardenas sat in Ricardo's office. It was just after eight on Monday night. Both men were in their three-piece business suits. Ricardo leaned back in his chair and said, "the gala is in two weeks." Julian said "I can't believe it's that time again. It seems like yesterday we were at the last gala." Julian and Ricardo had attended the same college. Ricardo had been the valedictorian and Julian had been right behind him. Both men had done quite well. Ricardo came from a family of lawyers and CEOs. He was the oldest of six, with three younger sisters and two brothers. Julian was the oldest of four. He had two younger sisters and a younger brother. He was the second in command now at Ortiz enterprises.

Chapter Seven

Two short weeks later, it was time for the Delaisa festival. It was held every year to raise money for the local children's hospital. This year for the first time, it was being held at the Delaisa Grand Hotel. It was an opportunity for all the citizens of Delaisa to come together and socialize. The people of Delaisa were extremely hardworking and deserved to have a good time.

Chapter Eight

On the morning of the gala, Barbara Tompkins was bustling around the Delaisa Grand Hotel. This was her first year overseeing the grand event. As she stood in the grand foyer, she looked around. There was a huge white marble table in the middle with a huge bouquet of white roses. There was a huge chandelier over the table and there were purple, red and turquoise tapestries that hung on the walls. There were two staircases that led to the upstairs. She walked into the huge grand ballroom where workers were setting up tables.

Promptly at seven, the guests started to arrive. Carlo and Evelina Cecchi pulled up. Carlo looked quite handsome, dressed in his dark burgundy tuxedo and matching shoes. His dark brown hair was combed back. Evelina looked beautiful, with her long strawberry-blond hair styled in a waterfall braid. Soon after David and Miriam arrived with their good friends, Fabrizio and Rebeca Castillo and Benito and Noemi Cardona. All six were beautifully dressed.

As they walked into the grand ballroom, Noemi said to Benito "what a gorgeous room!" Benito nodded and said, "yes, it is." the six found their table. Little by little, the room started to fill up. David and Miriam Rivera arrived with their very good friends, Fabrizio and Rebeca Castillo. The four often went out together. The two women had grown up next door to each other and had attended the same college.

At eight o clock the party was in full swing. Everybody was in a great mood. People were walking around and mingling, and the band was playing some lively tunes.

During dinner, Dante made his way over to Roberto Valencia. Roberto was one of Duvan's most loyal clients. Enter bad boy Alessio Delaisa. Alessio looked extremely handsome, dressed in his trademark dark blue tuxedo and matching shoes. His jet black hair was combed back. As he walked to his table, several young ladies turned to look at him.

He sat with his parents, Stephani and Concetta. Concetta looked lovely in a long red gown with matched red sequined high-heeled sandals. Her long strawberry blond hair was in flowing curls. Stephani looked handsome in a deep burgundy tuxedo, white shirt and burgundy tie. His dark brown hair was combed back. Across from the Delaisa's were Julian Cardenas and Ricardo Ortiz. Julian was wearing his trademark dark purple tuxedo, white shirt and purple tie. Ricardo wore a black tuxedo, dark blue shirt and red tie. Both men looked extremely handsome.

Chapter Eleven

It was just after midnight when the guests started to slowly make their way out. Several guests had made reservations and went up to their rooms. Chiara and Marisa Cecchi and their good friends, cadence Ortega and Reyna Sierra went up to their room. They hung out late talking about cute boys and eating snacks. At this time, Alessio Delaisa and Blanca Cardona went up to his room. The two talked late into the night. They discovered that they had a lot in common. As it turns out, they both wanted the same things in life. For Alessio, it was refreshing to finally find a girl who had dreams. For Blanca, she liked what she saw in Alessio. It was only after three in the morning when the two went to sleep.

Chapter Twelve

Two days later, Dante found the courage to call Olivia Valencia. Since the night of the gala, she had been on his mind.

when she answered, his heart skipped a beat. He said in his sexy velvet voice “hello Olivia.” she smiled to herself as she sat at the kitchen counter. She was surprised but pleased to hear from him. She said, “hello Dante.” he said to Olivia “I have been thinking about you.” she replied “I’m glad you called.” after a brief silence, he asked her “are you free for dinner tonight?” Olivia said “yes, I am.” Dante said “great. I’ll pick you up at seven thirty. There is a new restaurant I’ve been wanting to try.” Olivia said, “I look forward to seeing you.” Dante said, “I do too.” as soon as she hung up from Dante, she went over to her closet. All her dresses now seemed outdated. Picking up her purse, she headed out. Olivia Valencia was smart and hardworking and good to her parents.

Chapter Thirteen

Meanwhile Alessio Delaisa sat across from his father in his office. One of the topics of discussion was Alessio one day taking over Delaisa enterprises.

Stephani Delaisa was a man who demanded excellence from his staff, and he rewarded them well. After graduating at the top of his class from a well-known university, he had continued on to get his MBA. Now he was the powerful CEO of Vecchio enterprises. He secretly hoped that one day, Alessio would take over the reigns. Stephani said to Alessio, “one day I expect you to run my company.” Alessio, seated across from him said “I have my own company to run.” it was the same conversation the two always had. Alessio was a bit of a bad boy. He was also very driven and hardworking. He had his own plans and ambitions for his life.

Chapter Fourteen

On Friday night, all Alessio wanted was to spend time with Bianca Cardona. On the night of the gala, the two had hit it off. As Alessio sat in his living room, he pulled out his cell phone and called Bianca. As soon as she answered, he said "hey baby. I need to see you." she replied "I was just thinking about you."

After a brief silence, he asked her "are you free for dinner tonight?" Bianca replied, "yes. I am." Alessio said, "great. I'll pick you up at seven." Bianca said, "that sounds good." promptly at seven that evening, Alessio pulled in front of Bianca's apartment. He pulled out his phone and called her. She quickly grabbed her sweater and purse and dashed out the door. Alessio was standing against his car. He opened the door for her. As they were driving, she asked him "so where are we going?" he said "It's a surprise." a few minutes later, they arrived at a restaurant. As they were walking in, Alessio reached for Bianca's hand. There was a sense of intimacy walking hand in hand. The restaurant was not too crowded. There was a relaxed atmosphere.

People sat at nearby tables engaged in quiet conversation.

After they placed their orders, Bianca made her way to the ladies room. Over dinner, Bianca and Alessio talked about their childhood. It was minutes to ten when Bianca glanced at het watch. She said to Alessio "I didn't realize it was that late." Alessio looked at his watch and said, "oh wow. Let's get going." as they were walking to his car, Bianca said to Alessio, "I had a great time tonight." Alessio said, "so did I."

Chapter Fifteen

Over the next few months things were pretty quiet in Delaisa. Dante Cecchi and Olivia were enjoying their relationship. Alessio and Bianca were having a great time. The two had gone away together, during which their relationship deepened. For Bianca, it was the first time in her life that a good man actually wanted to be with her. For Alessio, it had been a long time since he had been happy in a relationship. Neither wanted to rush things. Alessio wanted to take things slow with Bianca and let things develop naturally.

A ghost from Dante's past was about to make her appearance, Bianca Delaisa. The story was a few years before Dante and Bianca had been in an extremely passionate relationship. Bianca had expected that she and Dante would have gotten engaged. Just the night when she had been hoping that he would propose to her, he had completely blindsided her by abruptly ending their relationship. As Bianca sat in her living room now, she thought back to that final night. She and Dante had gone out for dinner. Not long after they got back to his apartment, he had said "I feel it's time we break up." Bianca had thought she had heard wrong. Then he fed her the usual line "It's not you, it's me." Bianca had felt several emotions at once; hurt, anger and disappointment. She stood up and said to Dante" you really are a world class bastard." with that, she stormed out of his apartment and slammed the door.

Chapter Seventeen

Enter GianCarlo Saachi. GianCarlo was the senior editor of Saachi publishing. GianCarlo had very recently moved to Delaisa. Two months before, he had broken with his girlfriend of eight years. Now he was ready for a fresh start. As he arrived in town, he took note of all the little shops. GianCarlo Saachi was very driven and very philanthropic. He enjoyed donating a generous sum of money to several charities. As he had done very well for himself, he felt the need to give back.

It was Friday night and the happening place to be was the trendy new nightclub owned by Evelio and Juliana Suarez. It was just after eight and the place was hopping. GianCarlo Saachi walked in and made his way over to a far table. As he was sipping his beer, he took note of a certain young lady as she came in. After a while he slowly made his way over to her. He said in his low sexy voice "well hello, young lady." she smiled at him and asked him" have we met before?" he said "no. Please allow me to introduce myself. I am GianCarlo Saachi. And you are?" she said "I am Chiara Cecchi." Chiara Cecchi had had bad luck with men. Now she told herself to be careful. She was smart and hardworking.

The one area of her life where she had so far had trouble was in her love life. Too many times she had had her heart broken by a tall handsome stranger. Now she told herself to be careful.

Chapter Nineteen

A few days later, as GianCarlo Saachi sat at his desk, he thought about Chiara. There was something about her that intrigued him. He found himself wanting to learn more about her. Part of him was still not fully over his ex. Although he had been the one to end the relationship, he still sometimes missed her. So now he felt the need to hold back with Chiara. GianCarlo hoped that in time he would be able to fully commit to Chiara. For now, the two were having a good time. GianCarlo had learned from his past relationships that things had to develop naturally.

Chapter Twenty

It was the holiday season in Delaisa, and the town was bustling. Everybody was in a good mood. The town was nicely decorated. The major excitement was the upcoming Christmas gala; which would be held at the Delaisa grand hotel in two weeks. The holidays were always a festive time in Delaisa. There were red and green decorations everywhere and there was a large Christmas tree right in the town square that would be lit on Christmas Eve, during a festive ceremony.

Chapter Twenty-One

Bianca Delaisa had just arrived in town. After the unexpected break up with Dante, she had felt the need to get away. Now she was back and determined to get him back. The fact of the matter was that she hadn't gotten over him. There were several times during the last few weeks of their relationship when she thought he was going to propose. She had even made quiet mention to her family that a proposal was on the horizon.

It was a guys night out for Carlo Cecchi, Roberto Valencia, Carmelo Cardenas and Patricio Osorio. It had been a while since the four men had hung out. All four men were in the world of finance. The four men had met on their first day at a well-known university. Now all four had done quite well. Carlo Cecchi had a lot to be proud of. His two daughters were doing quite well. One was a writer and the other owned her boutique. His son, Dante was a certified financial planner at his own financial firm. Carmelo Cardenas and his wife, Patricia had a very successful and loving marriage. The same was true for Patricio Osorio and his wife, Marta. Roberto Valencia was the proud husband to Viviana. Together they had three children who were very successful; Francisco, Olivia and Rosalia.

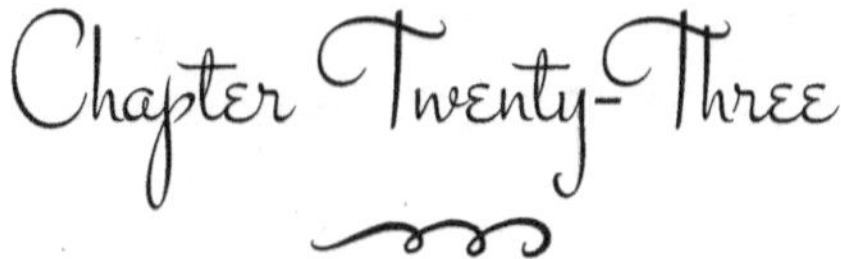

Two weeks later, it was time for the Charity Gala. This year it was being held at the Delaisa Grand Hotel. The Delaisa Grand Hotel was just five years old. It was well designed. As one entered the hotel, one would see the double staircases that led to the five hundred guest rooms. In the middle of the grand foyer was a huge black and white marble table on which was a huge vase with four dozen long stem pink and white roses. Across from the concierge desk was a big, lovely gift shop, where one could find several items; from key chains to mugs, pens and shirts. Upstairs, the guest rooms were quite spacious. On the top floor were the executive offices.

Chapter Twenty-Four

Promptly at seven thirty, the guests started to arrive. Giorgio and Felicita Saachi arrived in Giorgio's very expensive new car. As they walked in to the Delaisa Grand Hotel, they were greeted by Daniel Tomas. Daniel was overseeing the gala. Daniel looked extremely handsome dressed in his dark blue tuxedo with crisp white shirt and dark blue shoes. His curly black hair was combed back. Slowly the Other guests started filing in. Daniel showed them the way to the grand ballroom. The grand ballroom was set with forty tables on each side. In the middle of the grand ballroom was the dance floor. Daniel's cousin Felipe Casari was the DJ.

It was on this occasion that Bianca Delaisa decided to make her presence known. As she walked in, she spotted Dante Cecchi across the room. He looked quite handsome in his trademark dark purple tuxedo with a black lapel, white shirt and black tie. He was sitting beside a young lady. His parents were seated across from him. Bianca sat at a far table. During the evening, she would occasionally glance over at Dante. He seemed to be quite taken by his new girl. He could see him looking at his girl with affection. Bianca thought to herself, he used to look at me like that.

By nine the party was in full swing. Dinner had just been served and everybody was in a great mood. People were getting ready for Christmas and eagerly anticipating the new year. Dinner was a selection of roasted garlic chicken with broccoli, grilled salmon and mixed vegetables, or filet mignon.

During dinner, people were engaged in conversation. Meanwhile, the band was playing not too loud. There was an air of festivity. Not long after dinner, dessert was served. The band played some lively tunes and people made their way to the dance floor.

As it turns out, David and Miriam Rivera were both great dancers. Quite soon the dance floor was full.

Chapter Twenty-Six

It was just after midnight when the guests started to slowly make their way out. Several of the guests made their way up to their rooms.

An hour later, the hotel was still and quiet. It was in the early morning hours Felipe laid awake. He glanced at his watch which read 6:30. He got out of bed and made his way over to the window. From where he stood, he could see the bright lights of Delaisa. After several minutes, he went back to bed. It wasn't long before he fell into a deep sleep.

Chapter Twenty-Seven

It was after four o'clock in the morning when GianCarlo and Chiara fell asleep. The two had talked late into the night. It was just after seven that morning when GianCarlo woke up. He looked over at Chiara, who was still fast asleep. He very quietly slipped out of bed and went over to the window. The day was overcast and rainy. Just then Chiara opened her eyes and looked GianCarlo. She said, "good morning, Gianni." he turned and smiled at her. Sitting beside her, he leaned over and kissed her. At first the kiss was playful, then their kisses deepened. He had her in his arms and their passion for each other swept over them. Her arms were around his neck. As things got hotter between them, it was Chiara who said "let's not do it here and now. Let's wait." GianCarlo, ever the gentleman, though disappointed, said "well, okay. "Chiara kissed his cheek.

As fabulous as the Delaisa Grand Hotel appeared, it had a most unpleasant secret. Daniel Tomas as it turns out, was a most curious young man. One day not long after the gala, Daniel found himself wandering around. He just happened to come to a hidden door. As he opened the door, there was a sudden gust of wind. He closed the door behind him and went slowly down the steps. Each step creaked under his feet. He felt a sense of excitement with each passing moment. As he reached the bottom step he turned to his left. He went a few feet then he came to the double doors. Opening the doors he reached for the light switch. With the large room brightly lit, he walked in, not sure what he was seeing. There were countless filing cabinets.

It was the first time he had been down there. Now his curiosity was piqued. He tried cabinet after cabinet, and all were locked. What could possibly be in these cabinets, he wondered to himself. Daniel had no way of knowing that if he were to see what was in the files, it could possibly change his life. As he glanced at his watch, he saw it was getting late. He quickly made his way back and upstairs. He made a mental note to himself to go back. Unbeknownst to him, in his haste to get out of the basement, he had dropped his i.d. badge.

Chapter Twenty-Nine

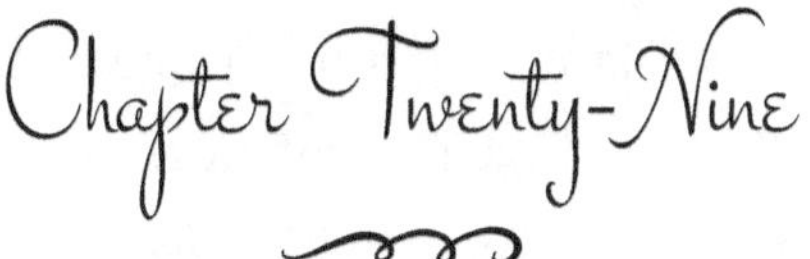

A few days nights after the gala, GianCarlo sat in his home office, thinking about Chiara. He had to admit to himself that there was something about her that intrigued him.

He suddenly found himself wanting to get to know her better. He took out his phone and called her. When she answered, his heart skipped a beat. He said softly "I was hoping I'd get you." she smiled to herself. She was surprised but pleased to hear from him.

Since the gala, he had been on her mind. He asked her "are you free for dinner tonight?" Chiara said " yes, I am." GianCarlo said " great. I'll pick you up at seven."

Chapter Thirty

Late Friday night, Daniel Tomas and his girlfriend Rosalia Valencia were relaxing in his new apartment. They had just gotten back from a lovely dinner. Due to their busy schedules, it had been a while since they had spent some time together. Although they were only four months into their relationship, Daniel felt that Rosalia might be the one for him. He had had a few girlfriends in the past. Something was different with him and Rosalia. Rosalia was enjoying being with Daniel. He was unlike the men she had dated previously.

Chapter Thirty-One

Stephani Delaisa had a dark secret. It was a secret that if it came out could ruin his family. The story was; several years before, he had had a very passionate love affair with Felicita Saachi. It was during a rough patch in his marriage.

One night, Stephani had had a huge fight with his wife, Concetta. They had both said things they could not take back. Stephani had stormed out of their apartment. He went into a bar. While he was there, he met a young lady, Felicita Saachi. Over drinks the two had talked about their lives. After a few hours, Felicita said to him "I should get going." Stephani glanced at his watch and said "oh, I didn't realize it was that late." still not wanting to go home, he said to Felicita, "let's go somewhere and continue our talk." Felicita said, "I'd like that." they went to the Delaisa grand hotel, owned by Stephani Delaisa.

Once they had gone up to a bedroom, Felicita laid down on the bed. Stephani came and sat beside her. He leaned over and kissed her. At first the kiss was playful. Then their kisses deepened. It wasn't long before their clothes were in a heap on the floor. Felicita was quite pleased to see that not only did Stephani Delaisa know what to do in the bed, but he did it quite well, four times. Afterward, the two laid together, both quite tired but very satisfied. So their love affair began. While Concetta Delaisa was at home, every night Stephani and Felicita were having relations in their hotel room. During their love affair, they wrote very intimate letters to each other. As it turns out, Stephani had kept all their love letters safe in filing cabinets in the basement of the Delaisa grand hotel.

Now as Stephani sat in his office, he thought about the extremely passionate love letters he and Felicita wrote to each other. Picking up his keys and jacket, he left his office. He decided to go down to the basement. At this time of night, everyone was settled. He slowly made his way down to the basement. As he got to the huge double doors, he felt a sudden gust of cool air. He walked past the filing cabinets. He stopped at one cabinet. Reaching into his jacket pocket, he pulled out his key. As he opened the drawer, he pulled out a file.

Meanwhile, Daniel Tomas' curiosity was getting the better of him. All day he had been trying to get back to the basement. He glanced at his watch. It was just after ten. Why not ? he thought to himself. As he was making his way to the basement, he wondered where his name badge had disappeared to.

He very quietly made his way to the basement. As soon as he got to the double doors, he realized someone was there. Not wanting to be seen, he very quickly and quietly turned around. While Stephani was looking over a file, he heard a noise. He quickly looked up and called out" who's there?" not hearing anything, he turned his attention back to the file.

Chapter Thirty-Three

Felicita Saachi had a secret. While she and Stephani Delaisa were passionately involved, she had conceived. Nine months later, in a private hospital, she had given birth to beautiful baby boy. As she now sat in her kitchen, she wondered as she often did where her son was. She privately hoped for the day when she and her son would be reunited.

Chapter Thirty-Four

Daniel Tomas could remember little if anything about his childhood. He often wondered who his parents were. Now as an adult, he felt the desire to know his parents.

Daniel Tomas was quite intelligent and very driven. After graduating from a top university, he had found the position of event planner at the Delaisa grand hotel. Now he was doing quite well for himself. He hoped for the day when he would finally find his Mrs. Right. There had been a few times in the past when he thought he had found the right girl, but things didn't work out.

Chapter Thirty-Five

It was a girl's night out for Natalia Rivera, Antonella Castillo, Sofia Salazar and Ilaria Delaisa.

It had been a while since the four girls had hung out. All four were quite busy with their respective careers. Natalia Rivera was doing well with her boutique. In fact, she was looking about moving to a bigger location. Antonella Castillo had just finished recording her debut album. So she was very excited. Sofia Salazar had just come back from her book tour and her best friend, Ilaria Delaisa had just finished writing her debut novel and was looking for a publisher.

Enter tall handsome Christian Grant. Christian was the powerful CEO of grant enterprises. After graduating from a top university with his bachelor's in economics, he had continued on to get his MBA. At the age of twenty five, he had started his company. Christian grant was very generous. He enjoyed donating money to local charities. He was also very kind to his parents. Two months before, Christian had ended an eight year relationship. Now he was looking for a fresh start. As he came into town, he took note of all the little shops.

Chapter Thirty-Seven

It was a hot night in Delaisa and the happening place to be was trendy new night club, Delancy. As it was Friday night, the place was hopping. As newcomer Christian Grant walked in, several young ladies turned to look at him.

Christian looked very handsome. He was wearing his dark blue suit, white shirt and red tie. His dark brown hair was combed back. As he was walking to his table, he heard a familiar voice. When he turned around, he was surprised to see Philip Amory. He and Philip had attended the same college. Philip said to him "well, well. I haven't seen you in a long time." Christian said "yeah. I know it's been too long." the two men sat at a corner table. After a few hours, Philip glanced at his watch and said "wow, I should get going." Christian said "yeah. I should head out now too." as they were walking to their cars, Philip said to Christian, "we should hang out again." Christian said, "yeah we should."

A few months later it was once again fall in Delaisa and the leaves were changing. It was getting quite cool. People were already looking forward to Thanksgiving, which was two weeks away. Everyone knew that once Thanksgiving came, Christmas was not far away.

In a few weeks, the town would be beautifully decorated. In Delaisa, the holidays were a time for many to reflect on the past year and to look expectantly to the new year. The holidays were also a time for families to get together.

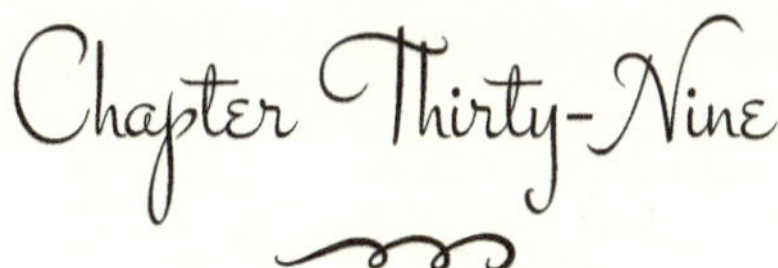

Chapter Thirty-Nine

A few short weeks later, it was December and people in Delaisa were starting to get into the holiday spirit.

All the stores were decorated with red and green, and a huge Christmas tree was already in the town square for all to see. On Christmas eve, it would be lit. On that night, all the citizens of Delaisa would be out and about. Christmas eve in Delaisa was a time for everyone to come celebrate and have a good time.

Natalia Rivera was especially looking forward to the upcoming holiday season. It was when she did the best business. She had just gotten in new merchandise that she expected would be a hit.

Stephani Delaisa laid awake thinking about Felicita Saachi. The fact was for the past two months, she had been on his mind constantly. He found himself thinking back to when they were involved. Stephani had never really gotten over Felicita. There had been times during their time together when he thought he might be in love with Felicita. He glanced over at his wife, who was sound asleep. He quietly slid out of bed and slowly made his way to the kitchen. He glanced at his watch. It read 9:25. Not too late, Stephani thought to himself. After glancing quickly down the hall, he called Felicita. When she answered, he felt his heart skip a beat.

Bright and early on Sunday morning, Stephani Delaisa and Felicita Saachi sat together at a corner table in the new cafe. Felicita knew this was the right time for her to tell Stephani about his son. After taking a long sip of coffee, she said to Stephani, "I have to tell you something." Stephani asked her "what is it?" Felicita said, "while we were together, I became pregnant." Stephani sat up straight in his chair and said, "go on." Felicita said, "we have a son." Stephani sat quiet for a long moment. Finally, he asked her "why didn't you tell me back then?" Felicita replied, "I wasn't sure how you'd react." after a brief silence, she asked him, "are you mad at me?" Stephani took a deep breath then said "no I am not. I'm just surprised." he reached his hands across the table and took hers. He said to her "I want to know our son. What is his name?" Felicita said, "I named him after my father and your father; Daniel Tomas."

Chapter Forty-Two

All day Stephani was trying to come to terms with what Felicita had told him. Now as he sat in his living room, he tried to do the math on how old Daniel is. A few minutes later, Stephani knew what he had to do. He grabbed his phone, keys and jacket and left. As soon as he got to the hotel, he raced down to the basement. As he entered the huge room, he saw Daniel Tomas standing in front of a filing cabinet. Stephani asked him "what are you doing here?" Daniel replied "I am trying to get into this cabinet. I am trying to find out who my parents are." Stephani said to him "Daniel, we need to talk." he opened the drawer and after locating the right file, he pulled it out. He turned to Daniel and said, "let's go up to my office." the two men went up to Stephani's office. As it turns out, Felicita was standing at the door. The three of them went into Stephani's office and closed the door. Once the three were seated,

Stephani said to Daniel, “I have to tell you something.” just then, Felicita cleared her throat. Both men glanced at her. Stephani said, “we have to tell you something.” as he reached over and took Felicita’s hand, he said to Daniel, “I am your father, and this is your mother.” Felicita looked at Daniel and nodded. Daniel sat up straight in his chair, shocked at what he had just been told. After all these years of wondering who his parents were, here he now sat with them. It was a lot to process for him. After a long silence, he said to Stephani “you’re my father.” Stephani nodded. Daniel looked at Felicita and said, “you’re my mother.” Felicita nodded. After a few minutes, he asked Stephani “do I have any siblings?” Stephani leaned back in his chair and said “yes. You do. You have a brother and two sisters.”

Chapter Forty-Three

A few short weeks later, it was Christmastime. Everybody was getting ready for the huge Christmas ball. It was to be held at the newly built, Grant Hotel.

The grant hotel was nestled on a hill that overlooked Delaisa. There were over five hundred rooms. As soon as one entered the hotel, one would see the huge black and white marble table in the middle. On the table was a huge vase of three dozen long stem white roses. Over the table was a huge chandelier. At the far end were twin winding staircases that led to the guest rooms.

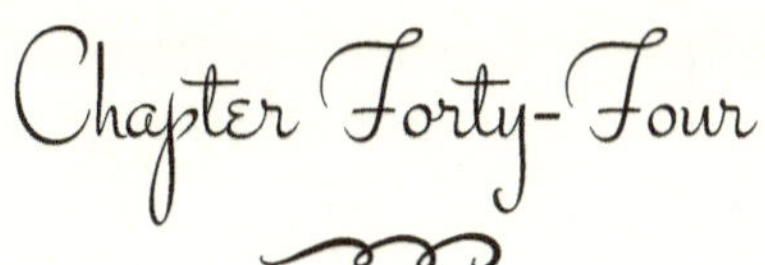

Chapter Forty-Four

The guests started to arrive promptly at seven thirty. Christian Grant arrived with his new girlfriend. Christian looked extremely handsome dressed in his trademark dark gray suit, white shirt and black tie. His dark brown hair was combed back. Not long after, Dante Cecchi arrived with his parents, Carlo and Evelina. GianCarlo Saachi walked in with Chiara on his arm. The two had now been together for four months and things were going quite well. The servers were walking around with trays of hor deurves. Among the guests, was a handsome stranger. As he came in, several turned to look at him. He was tall and quite handsome. He made his way over to a far table and sat down.

Chapter Forty-Five

By nine the party was in full swing. Everybody was in a great mood. The band was playing some lively Christmas songs. Halfway through the evening, the band left, and Felipe Casari took over as DJ. Felipe was 5'8 and extremely handsome. He was a bit of a bad boy. Not many people knew that he could be very romantic. Everybody was moving around and mingling. Some people sat in small groups. At eight o clock, dinner was served.

During dinner, GianCarlo Saachi made his way over to Carlo and Evelina Cecchi. It was a good opportunity for people to catch up with each other.

Chapter Forty-Six

It was just after midnight when the guests started to slowly make their way out. Some of the guests had made reservations and went up to their rooms.

GianCarlo Saachi and Chiara Cecchi went up to their room. As soon as they entered, Chiara laid down on the bed. GianCarlo came over and sat beside her. He leaned over and kissed her. At first the kiss was playful and light. Then their kisses deepened.

For GianCarlo Saachi, it had been a long time since he had felt like this. After his last breakup, he had told himself that it would be a long time before he would open his heart again. There was something about Chiara that drove him wild. For Chiara, it was the first time that a good man had looked her way. She was starting to see in herself what GianCarlo saw. The fire between them was blazing.

Chapter Forty-Seven

Over the next few months, things were pretty quiet in Delaisa. The new year had come and gone, and people were just going about their daily routine.

With the holidays now over, things were quiet in Delaisa. There was a buzz around town as to who the mysterious stranger at the Christmas gala was. Several guests at the Christmas gala had taken note of him, especially several women. At the local beauty salon, the talk was about that mysterious hunk at the gala.

Chapter Forty-Eight

Felipe Casari stood at his window staring out. Since the night of the gala, Kaia Londono had been on his mind. During the gala, Kaia Lodono had caught Felipe Casari's eye. It hadn't been until the end of the night when Felipe finally got the chance to speak to her. Just as he approached her, some of her friends had called her away. Felipe had no way of knowing that at that exact moment, Kaia was thinking about him. He took out his cell phone and called her. On the second ring, she said "hello?" Felipe said "hey baby girl. It's Felipe." Kaia smiled to herself. She said "hey Felipe. What's going on?" Felipe said "not much. I was just thinking about you." Kaia said, "you've been on my mind too." Felipe asked her "are you free for dinner tonight?" Kaia replied, "yes I am." Felipe told her "I'll pick you up at seven." Kaia said, "sounds good." Felipe arrived promptly at seven that night. They went to a most delightful new restaurant.

Over dinner Felipe said to her “you look very beautiful tonight.” Kaia smiled and said “thanks, you look very handsome.” after dinner, they went back to Felipe’s new apartment. As they walked in, Kaia looked around and said to Felipe, “you have a really nice place.” Felipe said, “thank you.” he went into his kitchen and poured two glasses of champagne. Kaia and Felipe sat together on his couch. An hour later, Kaia glanced at her watch and said to Felipe, “I should get going.” Felipe looked at the clock on the mantelpiece and said “wow, I didn’t realize it was that late.” he said to Kaia, “why don’t you stay with me tonight?” Kaia thought for a minute then said “oh, ok.” the fact was she was in no hurry to leave Felipe. As she settled into his bed, he laid down on his couch. Both laid awake thinking about the other.

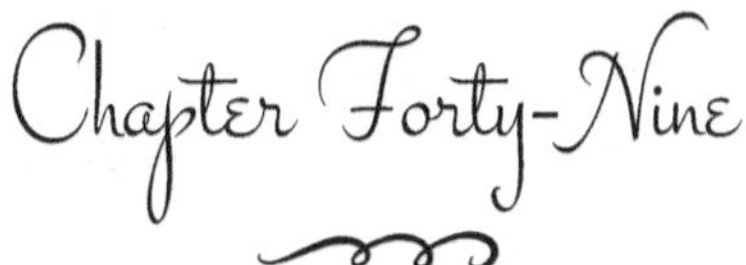

On a Friday night, Felipe Casari and Kaia Londono had just gotten back to his apartment after a lovely dinner in a fancy new restaurant. Felipe pulled Kaia into his arms and kissed her. At first the kiss was light and playful, then their kisses deepened. It wasn't long before they made their way to his bedroom. Soon after, clothes were on a pile on the floor. An hour later, Kaia Londono came to know only too well that not only did Felipe Casari know what to do in the bed, but that he did it well, four times. Afterward, they laid together, quite tired and both very satisfied.

Felipe leaned over and kissed Kaia. Kaia felt a thrill run up her spine, but they were both tired by then. He pulled her into his strong, powerful, muscular arms. It wasn't long before they were fast asleep in each other's arms.

Chapter Fifty

On a cool night, there was a grand reunion between mother and son. Felicita stood face to face with her son; after all these many long years.

Although Felicita had imagined this moment for so long, she was at a complete loss for words once she saw her son. She held him for the longest time, never wanting to let go of him. Now she understood how those other mothers felt when they held their children. Standing now with Daniel in her arms, she was filled with great love and immense pride. For Daniel, it was the moment he never thought would come. He had always wanted to know his parents. Now here he was with his mother, finally. Both were weeping soft sobs of joy. After the longest time, Felicita said to Daniel, "we have so much to catch up on." Daniel nodded and said "yes, mom, we do." Felicita had never heard such beautiful words.

Six months later, Felipe Casari knew in his heart that he had found the one. It was the first time in his life he had felt this way about any girl. On a Friday night, after a romantic dinner, he and Kaia went back to his new apartment. Right after dessert, he knelt in front of Kaia. As Kaia looked into his shiny dark eyes, she knew the moment had finally come. She had been waiting for this moment for the last two months. Felipe took her hands in his and said "Kaia, I want you to know that I have fallen very deeply in love with you, and I love you more than anything. You have my heart forever will you marry me?" with tears in her eyes she nodded and said "yes, yes." Felipe reached into his jacket pocket, took out the ring and slid it onto her finger. It was a perfect fit. He pulled her into his arms, and they shared a very passionate kiss.

Chapter Fifty-Two

On a warm Saturday night, all of Delaisa was gathered at the Delaisa grand hotel. The occasion was the surprise engagement party for Felipe Casari and Kaia Londono. As Felipe and Kaia walked in, everyone cheered. It was a great night. Felipe held Kaia's hand as they walked around, greeting their guests. Both looked very happy, and everyone could tell that they were very deeply in love with each other.

He stood at a distance, just taking in the festivities. He did not want to be seen. What a happy bunch, he thought to himself as he watched the happy couple in the midst of all their guests. They won't be happy for too long. Just that thought brought a smile to his face.

www.ingramcontent.com/pod-product-compliance
Lightning Source LLC
LaVergne TN
LVHW090126160826
845673LV00015B/1034